Talking to the Dead

ELAINE FEINSTEIN was educated at Newnham College, Cambridge. She has worked as a university lecturer, a subeditor, and a freelance journalist. Since 1980, when she was made a Fellow of the Royal Society of Literature, she has lived as a full-time writer. In 1990, she received a Cholmondeley Award for Poetry, and was given an Honorary D.Litt from the University of Leicester. Her versions of the poems of Marina Tsvetaeva – for which she received three translation awards from the Arts Council – were first published in 1971 and remain in print. She has written fourteen novels, many radio plays, television dramas, and five biographies, including *Ted Hughes: The Life of a Poet*, shortlisted for the biennial Marsh Biography Prize. She has travelled extensively, not only to read her work at festivals across the world, but to be Writer in Residence for the British Council, first in Singapore, and then in Tromsø, Norway. She was a Rockefeller Foundation Fellow at Bellagio in 1998. Elaine Feinstein's poems have been widely anthologised. Her *Collected Poems and Translations* (2002) was a Poetry Book Society Special Commendation. She has served as a judge for the Gregory Awards, the Independent Foreign Fiction Award, and the Whitbread Poetry Prize, and in 1995 was chairman of the judges for the T.S. Eliot Prize. Her biography of Anna Akhmatova, *Anna of all the Russias*, was published in July 2005.

ELAINE FEINSTEIN

Talking to the Dead

CARCANET

Acknowledgements

Some of these poems have already appeared in *The Times Literary Supplement*, *PN Review*, *Poetry London* and *Poetry Review*.

First published in Great Britain in 2007 by
Carcanet Press Limited
Alliance House
Cross Street
Manchester M2 7AQ

A CIP catalogue record for this book is available from the British Library
ISBN 978 1 85754 902 7

The publisher acknowledges financial assistance from Arts Council England

Typeset by XL Publishing Services, Tiverton
Printed and bound in England by SRP Ltd, Exeter

In memory of Arnold Feinstein

Contents

Winter

The clock's gone back. The shop lights spill
over the wet street, these broken streaks
of traffic signals and white headlights fill
the afternoon. My thoughts are bleak.

I drive imagining you still at my side,
wanting to share the film I saw last night,
– of wartime separations, and the end
when an old married couple reunite –

*You never did learn to talk and find the way
at the same time*, your voice teases me.
Well, you're right, I've missed my turning,
and smile a moment at the memory,

always knowing you lie peaceful and curled
like an embryo under the squelchy ground,
without a birth to wait for, whirled
into that darkness where nothing is found.

Bremerhaven

Christmas in Bremerhaven. Every twig sheathed
in transparent ice like tubes of glass, each breath
steam as it left our lips.
I did not want to go to the fair.

You would have liked to poke through toys
even in freezing rain, and relished the stalls
of rich cakes, bought some German games,
but I did not want to be there.

Then, in a wooden booth where we took shelter,
my son and I drank *glühwein* and spoke of you.
He was still angry about childhood memories,
and, as he spoke, suddenly, you were there,

– one-off, sardonic and obstreperous –
as if we had conjured your hot presence
to stand for a moment solidly between us,
before you dissolved back into the air.

Home

When was it you took up that second stick,
and began to walk like a cross country skier?
Your glide developed its own politics.
Last July, you were able to stretch over
like an acrobat, to oil the garden table.
The patio faced south. It was high summer.

Coffee and grapefruit was the breakfast ritual,
or boiled eggs eaten from blue terracotta.
Our paradise, you called it, like a *gîte*
we might have chosen somewhere in Provence.
Neither of us understood you were in danger.
Not even when we called the ambulance:

you'd been inside so many hospitals,
ticking your menus, shrugging off jabs and scans
talking unstoppably to visitors –
your long crippling made you bitterly clever.
Humped on your atoll, and awash with papers
you often argued like an angry man.

This time, however, you were strangely gentle.
Your face lit up as soon as I arrived;
smiling, you shooed the nurses out, and said
Now go away, I'm talking to my wife.
You liked it, when I brought myself to say
seeing you was the high point of my day.

The nurses, pushed for time, hauled you about
and fixed the bed without much ceremony.
You spoke of *home*, as if you were ET,
and wanted me to fetch you in the car – as
I would have, if the staff nurse had concurred.
Darling, they brought you in like a broken bird.

Your shoulder blades were sharp beneath your skin,
a high cheekbone poignant against the pillow.
Yet neither of us spoke a word of death.
My love, you whispered, *I feel so safe with you.*
That Monday, while I phoned, you waited loyally
for my return, before your last breath.

A Visit

I still remember love like another country
with an almost forgotten landscape
of salty skin and a dry mouth. I think
there was always a temptation to escape
from the violence of that sun, the sudden
insignificance of ambition,
the prowl of jealousy like a witch's cat.

Last night I was sailing in my sleep
like an old seafarer, with scurvy
colouring my thoughts, there was moonlight
and ice on green waters.
Hallucinations. Dangerous nostalgia.
And early this morning you whispered
as if you were lying softly at my side:

Are you still angry with me? And spoke my
name with so much tenderness, I cried.
I never reproached you much
that I remember, not even when I should;
to me, you were the boy in Ravel's garden
who always longed to be good,
as the forest creatures knew, and so do I.

Hands

We first recognised each other as if we were siblings,
and when we held hands your touch
made me stupidly happy.

Hold my hand, you said in the hospital.

You had big hands, strong hands, gentle
as those of a Mediterranean father
caressing the head of a child.

Hold my hand, you said. *I feel
I won't die while you are here.*

You took my hand on our first aeroplane
and in opera houses, or watching
a video you wanted me to share.

Hold my hand, you said. *I'll fall asleep
and won't even know you're not there.*

Beds

Last night I wondered where you had found to sleep.
You weren't in bed. There was no one in your chair.

Through every window the white, full moon glared.
I walked into the garden, shivering:

'Where are you, my darling? You will catch cold.'
Waking, I let the daytime facts unfold.

Unsent Email

When I travel without you, I am no more
than a gaudy kite on a long umbilical.
My flights are tethered by a telephone line
to your Parker Knoll, where you wait
lonely and stoical.

About the Festival: there were no penguins
crossing the road on the North Island,
no whales in Wellington harbour.
The nearest land mass is Antarctica, and
the wind blows straight from there to New Zealand.

Katherine Mansfield lived here as a child
and I've bought gartered stockings in bright colours
to honour her in the character of Gudrun.
For you, I've bought a woollen dressing gown.
You were always home to me. I long for home.

Mackintosh

Your spirit comes to me in a mackintosh
scented with volatile esters from the lab.
No one remembers you now as I remember:
your voice still shy, your sentences unfinished.
We were living in two rooms over the bridge
somewhere in Mill Road with mice in the kitchen.

I have never been so happy, you told me when
your grant came through, and then began
to sit all night in the basement of Free School Lane
watching a fraction collector,
muffled up in the same mackintosh,
which was grimed at the pockets

and worn with the belt twisted. This you flung
over the end of our bed in the early morning.
We were clumsy, unfastidious, tender.
Your spirit comes to me now
in a mackintosh to remind me how
easily we loved when we were young.

Fox

He thinks this is his garden, the red fox
we saw this morning, under the Tuscan cypress.
He hardly stirred as we pulled up the sash.
And perhaps his confidence is justified.

Tomorrow, at twelve o'clock, we shall have
no further foothold on this leafy street,
the tall white room, these silvery birches
and our raspberry brambles

all, like the freehold, will have been transferred
to our Greek purchaser; while the fox
will still enjoy a comfortable summer
on a diet of squirrels, rats, and small birds.

Moving House

We used to travel light. Grandparents knew
how to pack up and go in a single night,
with house spirits in a shoe.
Three generations on, we've lost
the knack.

Watching, from bed, a full moon caught
by nets of leaves in a familiar tree
I thought
while we live here, a planetary fruit
belongs to me.

How can I bear to leave that glow behind?
Waking today, I laugh at the conceit;
the niche we make on earth is all we share.
As for the moon, we'll find
her everywhere.

Stuff

Here we came in hot July, with the treasures
of a whole life together shambled in boxes
to be unwrapped and set out in new places:
the ebon carving of Rama's wife, Sita,
each hair precisely cut, the puppets
from Prague, heavy art deco goblets,
a Sung fan discovered in South East Asia,
a cherry-wood flute player. You were

always eager to explore, and equally pleased
to investigate auction rooms or an Oxfam shop.
In a hardware store, you discovered elegance in
a simple tool for shaving slivers of cheese.
Even caches of paper clips and staplers
hold your presence, and the screws,
the Araldite stored under the stairs

you often used to mend the backs of chairs.
Not to speak of the iMac, in which your spirit
still continues: nets of thought intensely lived.
And most of all, in walnut drawers beneath
the table by our bed where once you kept
sleeping pills and indigestion tablets:
your hearing aid, your spectacles, your teeth.

Rain

The band of mourners shuffled out across
a field of mud past rows of marble slabs
to watch your wooden box
lowered into the earth, there to be lost
beneath the shovelled soil.
Who turned up? It doesn't matter now.
The ceaseless rain poured over all of us.

I remember the cold, and wanting to be
home again, but not much more.
A hand I held, a son supported me,
I listened to a good friend's eulogy…
My mind was numb. *What's happening?*
you asked me once in a high fever.
I reassured you then. Now I am dumb.

Hubble

Beyond the flow of metal and frozen gas,
where the furthest stars circle, let us imagine
a being without any need for
the molecules of life, some blue force
at work spinning creation

while the camera of the NASA telescope
searches the miraculous beauty of the skies.
Men at their monitors whoop in triumph below.
And the Lord God watches the delicate toy
measuring heavenly secrets

– the chemical organisation of comets,
the birth and death of stars –
touched by the reach of human ingenuity,
the innocent presumption of men's lives,
their ends that hold no joy.

Immortality

If I believed in an old-fashioned Paradise,
then you, my love, would still be talking in it.
There would be blue sky and a few clouds
seen through stone arches, as in
Raphael's *School of Athens*, with Diogenes
sprawled on the steps, and Plato in the likeness of da Vinci.
You could pursue them with your eager questions –
as you once challenged speakers at LSE.

It's not that I hope to find you there
myself, more that I cannot bear
it should be true as once you said:
We think. And learn to understand a bit.
And then we're dead...

A Match

You hated swank.

Even in flowers
you did not like flamboyance
preferring small blue
petals of rosemary
to flags and peonies.

I liked a bit of flash,
glittery clothes, immodest
dancing, some euphoria
always with Dorothy Parker's
knowledge of disaster.

All our worst faults we shared:
disorder, absentmindedness, neglect.
You asked me once: *How
did you get away with it?*
before concluding harshly:

You must have been a tank.

Skin

There was a time *before* we met as well
as this inexorable *after*. If I had not

found you, who would I have been?
A woman who could dance a stylish tango

fretted with too much wanting – sex, success –
spoilt, self-seeking, and a little shallow

distrusting what I could not understand. There were
so many men I cannot list them all.

Some I abandoned, some abandoned me.
One I loved well gave me a diamond –

I often wondered what happened to him –
Then you became the skin of all I am.

Flame

There must be something I still hope to find.
Honour, perhaps. I do not look for love.

We never said goodbye, though I remember
whispering to you in the Royal Free,

'You do know, I have loved you all my life?'
with a quick nod and smile your only answer.

Once you described me as *a natural spinster*,
meaning a loner, happiest on my own;

you knew that was not so. Once home from
hospital, you called me *wife* and *mother* –

that last was what you wished.
Will you take these poems from me now

as if they were Akhmatova's snowdrops,
or a flame in a clay dish?

Another Anniversary

Today is your birthday. There is cool sunshine.
Fig leaves and roses cover the wooden fence.
What happiness can I wish you in your death?

Here is the garden that I made for us
though you saw only the winter shape
of a weeping crab apple and a bare plum,

it was my offering, and you received it so;
but most of what we work at disappears.
Little we worry over has importance.

The greedy and the generous have the same end.
The dead know nothing of what we say to them.
Still, in that silence let me write: *dear friend.*

A Pebble on Your Grave

It's easy to love the dead.
Their voices are mild. They don't argue.
Once in the earth, they belong to us faithfully.

But do they forgive us?
Our crabby failure to understand
their complaints, our manifest indignation

at words of blame. Once, I remember
you broke off some angry
exchange to say unhappily:

*I don't want your silly grief
after I'm dead, it's now
I need your pity.*

Widow's Necklace

Friends try my stories on their teeth or
with a match: are they plastic or amber?

My children say I must have forgotten
how I used to turn to them so very often

repeating your words and begging reassurance.
Why should I now recall a loving presence?

But so I do: my story as a wife
is threaded on the string of my own life,

and when I touch those beads, I still remember
your warm back as we slept like spoons together.

Father and Son
A dream

One night in the multi-storey car park
near Jesus Green, it was silent and dark,

the lights were blown, the concrete
shoddy, no one about. Echoing feet

were walking towards my twelve-year-old son
who was dreaming that he held a soldier's gun;

this he fired many times at the sound
while the steps kept coming closer. Only then

did he make out the walking man was *you*,
now wounded to death. And still you threw

your arms out, as if to put them round
him, with a loving smile, before you fell to the ground.

Guernica

A motionless bull. An April afternoon.
No sky. No aeroplanes. Only
that screaming horse's tongue,
a triangle between distorted teeth;
the limp baby, an electric light bulb.
Familiar images, almost too well-known.

I stood in front of Picasso's painting
– now in Madrid – and remembered the print
you once stretched over a wooden frame,
and how in twenty years the bowsprit
warped and the paper yellowed
but you would not let me junk it.

You'd discovered the picture on your first visit
to the Museum of Modern Art fifty years ago.
It pleased you to study paintings on your own
without my often impatient company
– eager to move off and have a coffee –
Today I solemnly stand to look alone.

Folk Song

The songs of the anonymous delighted you:
people remembering them without PR,
singers like Woody Guthrie and Pete Seeger:
their music and words went into your library.

We were hiring a twin tub at five shillings a week
from a so-called friend, and when one day
we couldn't rustle up the rent to pay,
I let him nose about our books instead.

And off he went with your treasured
Alan Lomax anthologies in lieu.
Twenty years later you were still telling the story
as a bitter sign of how little I knew you.

Wittgenstein

Was it him in the Rex cinema,
that illicit afternoon, watching *Casablanca*
as another B movie? I wanted to believe it.
Nervously taking a short cut past
the bronze of Hermes once in Whewell's Court,

I saw him, though, of course, I did not speak.
Such timid gawking always made you impatient.
Meetings with thinkers were a serious matter. That's why
you hated to leave their presence, why you said unhappily:
Not enough people got to know me.

Afghan

My taxi driver yesterday was an Afghan
living in London for some years.
What he misses most, he explained, was
the sense that what he does matters to anyone.
There are no gains.

His neighbours rarely provoke him to more than
flickers of shame or occasional adrenalin.
He is in exile. Tonight I am alone,
simply a woman sitting undressed in
an Edward Hopper bedroom.

Restart

Would you like to restart your computer now?

Please, if you can, without erasing memory,
disabling software, or losing any files.

At my age, to begin again is more like starting a car
with leads for a jumpstart, or friends pushing:

the first cough falters, then you hear a rattle
as the engine fires. It is always a miracle.

Variation on an Akhmatova Poem

She drinks to her ruined home.
My own is not destroyed.
Still, the loneliness in marriage
is something I can toast.
I drink to your hostile stare,
our quarrels, your infidelity,
and what you resented most:
that God did not choose to save you,
and took some pity on me.

January Trees

Where shall I find the resilience of trees?
I envy their courage. In the first warm rain
the poplar branches swell with the hint
of new buds. There are even tips of yellow.

Have they have forgotten autumn, with last year's
chestnut leaves still rotten in the grass? That's not easy to do.
Let me study the endurance of my eucalyptus
whose ovals shivered in the wind all winter through.

Marriage

Is there ever a new beginning when every
word has its ten years' weight, can there be
what you call conversation between us?
Relentless you are as you push me
to dance and I lurch away from you
weeping, and yet can we bear to lie
silent under the ice together like
fish in a long winter?

A letter now from York is a reminder of
windless Rievaulx, the hillside moving through
limestone arches, in the ear's liquid the
whirr of dove notes: we were a fellowship of three
strangers walking in northern brightness, our
searches peaceful, in our silence the
resonance of stones only, any celibate
could look for such retreat, for me
it was a luxury to be insisted on
in the sight of those grass overgrown dormitories.

We have taken our shape from the
damage we do one another, gently as
bodies moving together at night, we mend
our gestures, softly we hold our places:
in the alien school morning in the
small stones of your eyes I know how
you want to be rid of us, you were
never a family man, your virtue is
lost, even alikeness deceived us
love, our spirits sprawl together
and both at last are distorted

and yet we go toward birthdays and other
marks   not wryly   not thriftily
waiting, for where shall we find it, a
joyous, a various world? in fury
we share, which keeps us, without
resignation: tender whenever we touch   what
else we share   this flesh we
bring together   it hurts to
think of dying as we lie close.

1969

Rosemary in Provence

We stopped the Citroën at the turn of the lane,
because you wanted a sprig of blue rosemary
to take home, and your coat opened awkwardly

as you bent over. Any stranger would have
seen your frail shoulders, the illness
in your skin – our holiday on the Luberon

ending with salmonella –
but what hurt me, as you chose slowly,
was the delicacy of your gesture:

the curious child, loving blossom
and mosses, still eager
in your disguise as an old man.

1997

Lazarus's Sister

On hot nights now, in the smell of trees and water,
you beg me to listen and your words enter my spirit.

Your descriptions unmake me; I am like wood
that thought has wormed; even the angels

that report our innermost wish must be kinder.
And yet, when your face is grey in the pillow, I wake you

gently, kissing your eyes, my need for you
stronger than the hope of love. I carry your body

where the hillside flickers: olive cypress ash.
But nothing brings relief. All our days

are numbered in a book. I try to imagine
a way our story can end without a magician.

1997

Lisson Grove

It is hot July, and sycamore wings lodge
in the windscreen wipers. In your illness,
you are begging me to make sense of your life,

and I am helpless as the single electric fan
whirring in the heat of your room
in the Charter Nightingale hospital.

At your bedside, I feel like someone
who has escaped too lightly
from the great hell of the camps,

except that I don't altogether escape,
when I open the door to the street:
the air is cooler, the sky night blue,

my shoes knock lonely notes from the pavement,
and two tramps salute my return to the car
with ironic cheers and cans of Special Brew.

1997

Separations

There's a whirr of wood pigeons this morning:
I should close the study window. Last spring
two of them tried to build their nest in the music;
big, stubborn birds you had to shift with a broom,
and as the pages fell to the floor I remembered
the scattered papers in that rented room,

when I stayed with you for the first time, and how
deeply we overslept, as if in finding each other
our dreams had joined at once in a single stream,
so we could escape the ordinary world, and
make common cause together like comrades
at the end of René Clair's *À nous la liberté*.

Ungainly, unworldly creatures we were,
two playing cards precariously leaning
and propping each other up, a friend observed.
But conversation was what you wanted,
some exchange of thought, while I
needed tenderness more than talk.

And so things often went wrong.
We were happy enough exploring the red light
district in Lille with a lonely Belgian crook, or taking
vodka and pilchards in a house of refuseniks
but at home both of us turned away. You
played music upstairs, I lived in my own song

or on the phone. Now, I've closed the study window.
This morning the sky is pale blue in the birch tree
and you lie asleep, your mouth hurt by last
night's squabble. Will we never escape
the need to sift through the long past together
in our effort to establish a new shape?

Bonds

There are owls in the garden and a dog barking.
After so many fevers and such loss,
I am holding you in my arms tonight, as if
your whole story were happening at once:
the eager child in lonely evacuation
waking into intelligence and then
manhood when we were first *copains*,
setting up tent in a rainy Cornish field, or
hitchhiking down to Marseilles together.

You were braver than I was and so
at your side I was never afraid, looking for
Dom 99 in the snows of suburban Moscow,
or carrying letters through Hungarian customs,
I learnt to trust your intuitions more than my own,
because you could meet Nobel laureates,
tramps and smugglers with the same confidence,
and your hunches worked, those molecular puzzles,
that filled the house with clay and wire models.

In the bad times, when like poor Tom Bowling,
you felt yourself gone for ever more,
and threw away all you deserved, you asked me
What was it all for? And I had no answer, then
or a long time after that madness;
nor can I now suggest new happiness,
or hope of good fortune, other than
staying alive. But I know that lying at your side
I could enter the dark bed of silence like a bride.

1997

Wheelchair

We've travelled on a bumboat on the green South China seas,
seen papaya, dates and coconuts in crotches of the trees
and in Hawker centres Singapore keep quietly policed
eaten hundred year old eggs and fishbrains wrapped in bamboo leaf.
We've seen coolies who sold goats' milk and the men who
plundered them
while the ghosts of Maugham and Coward haunt the new Raffles
hotel;

but the most surprising feature of the perils we have passed
is you've travelled in a wheelchair with your left leg in a cast.
Most people would have had more sense, but we were both
surprised
to find it rather soothing. And one day we surmised:
you needed an attention that I hardly ever pay
while I enjoyed the knowledge that you couldn't get away.

Now the generator flickers far inland in Campuhan
and we lie inside our cottage cooled remotely by a fan,
or take a bath among the ferns and tall hibiscus trees.
Green rice grows in the paddy fields, we pick the coffee beans.
And outside, parked and ready, sits the chair that takes you round
to explore in a contentment that we've only rarely found.

1997

Living Room

How can we make friends before one of us dies
if you quarrel with two fingers in your ears,
like a child? Things won't come our right now.
You think I don't love you. I won't argue.
Your angry sadness stings me into tears.
I think of your old coat, smelling of chemicals,
leant against long ago in the Everyman queue,

when you offered me those tender early
films that made our lips tremble, or else
the forgiven boy in the forest of Ravel's opera,
more touching to me than your verbal
skills or passion for the genius of gesture
in crayon, mime, *commedia dell'arte*.
It's love we miss, and cannot bear to lose.

I know you would much prefer I choose
intelligence to prize, but that has
always had its downside, your words
so often cut me down to size, I wonder
if some accident removed me first, whether
my writing days would count as evidence
that in my loss was little real to miss.

The likeliest end is that the bay tree left
to my attention, withers on the window sill,
and moths lay eggs in the lentils, while
still hurt by memories of you as gentle, I'll
look into a monitor for comfort, and cry
aloud at night in the hope somewhere
your lonely spirit might hang on and care.

2000

Perugia

for Michele

We were two middle-aged women on a trip
walking the hilly streets of an Umbrian city
and pondering our versions of the divine;
my usual Hebraic bleakness skewed
by Perugino's thirteen-year-old faces,

and the kind fiction of his human God. Two chefs
came out from their hot kitchen to flirt with us,
and tell us to wish on the first star,
since this was the festival of the local saint's day.
We both stared up at a pagan sky.

We should never ask for anything, but we do,
we do – if only blessing – when alone in our beds.
That is where we learn to resign our spirits to
the harsh starlight of Hubble's discoveries,
and hope for protection from an unknown power.

Old Poets

To be in their presence once was
a shot of adrenalin. Wrinkled or flaccid,
they still exuded pheromones. They seemed
already immortal; we saw their future glory
around their heads like haloes.

Even to stand in the cemeteries where they lay
gave us a frisson of joy. We were so sure
the words of their poems would last,
and that the next generation
would be equally in love with the past.

Letter to Ezra Pound

Dear Ezra, the melody of your line
breathed in my ear for all my writing life;
I loved the syllables of *Lustra* and *Cathay*,
even while knowing you would casually
have seen me done for as a child of nine.

That 'dream in peasants' eyes'. What shall I say?
You must have known of rooms stained
with the blood of partisans, musicians'
fingers broken by police, and Jews,
always Jews, possessions stolen, murdered anyway.

Mussolini took no interest in you. How pretend
those broadcasts were no more than opportunist?
The sneers figured in letters to old friends,
and fellow poets: Reznikoff. Zukovsky.
A little more than that provincial prejudice

Ginsberg said you confessed to in Rapallo.
And yet, those *Pisan Cantos*… you were gifted
above any. And young writers found you generous.
Pull down thy vanity. Socrates warned us
not to trust poets centuries ago.

Common Sense

Common sense was never my strongest point.
I always needed help to fix a fuse
or superglue a broken bowl together.
In other matters I was mutinous.

You assured me a secular age would forget us.
That God was dying out of the souls of men.
That the Enlightenment, the Haskalah, would save us.
I did not argue, but I didn't believe you.

In Basel I ate snails in garlic butter
and let my children have bacon for breakfast.
My conversation with God was secret and shamefaced.
But over the years, we revived a few traditions.

Seder

In the old country, they drank hot tea
with cubes of sugar in their mouth
and Easter was a hazardous time.
You were often grumpy as I prepared a Seder.

Now you are gone, I go out to buy
ingredients for *charoseth* with less pressure –
apples, raisins, walnuts, honey, wine –
and the meal is quieter. We still put out

Elijah's glass of Palwin no. 4
and open the door
to let in a stranger, or an angel,
      or perhaps an enemy.

Scattering

1

In the lands of Sepharad, on the River Tagus:
a town the colour of biscuit, a long horizon,
smooth, bare mountains, and beyond
the desert and a white sliver of moon.

It is the limestone city of Toledo, where
the Jews settled after Jerusalem
– silversmiths, traders, basket makers, scholars –
and Spain at first was happy to receive them.

In a Golden Age of restored hope:
houses were built with fountains in the courtyard;
men in their book-lined studies were translators
who brought the Greeks through Arabic to Europe.

But when they had to leave, with frightened eyes,
they bartered a house for a donkey,
a vineyard for a piece of cloth,
and nicknames followed them, like police spies.

2

And those who did not leave?
They turned to the Holy Cross,
though some lit candles on a Friday night
without remembering why,

and cooked in oil rather than lard;
others became fervent New Christians,
and married into the best families;
until the Inquisition began to inquire

more urgently into their old habits,
– for instance, if they did not light a fire
on Saturdays in a cold winter –
Neighbours gave evidence against the rich.

Most admitted their sins under torture, as
people will, and some were brought to blame
fellow *conversos* for their practices.
It did not help them to escape the flames.

Nor did the ignorant suffer any less.
Read how Elvira del Campo pleaded,
as they broke her arms, only to understand:
Tell me what I have done that I may confess.

3

In Muslim lands, the refugees were welcome.
– Maimonides in Cairo, merchants in Baghdad –
invited to Istanbul, they sold Turkish carpets
in a stone market built for them by the Sultan.

There were glasses of sweet tea for customers.
At home, tables were set with plump brown plums
and aromatic grasses, furniture inlaid
with mother of pearl, and chimneys backed

with Iznik blue tiles. Mathematical patterns,
and simple worship: Jews and Muslims
lived side by side in the Ottoman Empire
though Jews were always second-class citizens.

From Smyrna came the false Messiah,
Shabbatai Zevi. He seduced the faithful
from Amsterdam to the *stetls* of Lithuania,
– until he bought his own life with apostasy.

Many of his followers turned to Islam;
of those some were *donmeh,* Jews in secret.
And they invented new stories for Karagoz, the wily
shadow puppet with a theatre of phantoms.

4

Not so easy in the lands of Ashkenaz.
Winter. Snow. Trees. An acrid smell
of gunpowder in the wind.
Not many Jews in Vienna's First District:

bankers paid a heavy tax for the privilege.
Those with beards and caftans came for the Fairs
and, when times were hard, they set up
market stalls near Leopoldstrasse

selling trinkets, second-hand goods or
potato cakes with sour pickles.
Emancipation let them be newspaper editors,
scribblers and soldiers. In a Hapsburg Empire

stretching through Budapest into Galicia
for all the ambiguities, Jews were loyal.
Assimilation would have been
honourable then, if it had been possible.

Let us not speak of Germany.
The best loved, the most murderous…

5

When Herman Melville visited Palestine
he saw a desolate landscape bleached
like bones, no moss, just naked stones
with lime ash in between them.

The Jewish stores then only sold rice,
or dingy looking sugar and dried fish.
Pale faced women were gnarled
as olive trees and carried sickly children.

Everywhere he saw sand and cactus.
Only the Bedou riding in from the desert
in flowing robes on camels stirred his blood.
Otherwise the land was not glamorous

hardly inviting settlement, even
for those caught in Kishinyov, still less
in Western Europe, before
the conviction of Captain Dreyfus.

6

I remember the broken bodies aboard
rotting ships turned back by the British:
how the young swam for the shore,
and the old preferred to drown.

I drank green tea with my Moroccan lover,
looking across barbed wire in Jerusalem.
At the end of that street were Jordanian guns.
No one expected Israel to survive.

In Gesher Ha-Zeev I was covered
with mosquito bites and afraid of spiders
living in the banana plants, but at night
we danced and I wore Yemenite silver.

Five wars later, Yehudah Amichai
told me in his house in Yemen Moshe:
I am completely unapologetic. Why
should I feel guilty for being here

writing poems and still hoping for peace?
I had to confess that in London, the same people
who once sent their children to work on kibbutzim
have begun to question Israel's right to exist.

Bruges

Canals. Cobbles. Bridges. Glinting sunshine.
My companion finds Bruges a decorous city.
– Perhaps too quiet, I murmur thoughtfully.
Still, there are bombers in London,
and policemen on the streets, while here
young people have the soft Flemish faces

Hans Memling liked to paint. My friend
remains courteous, even when he finds
my words – 'disaster', for instance –
inappropriate to our situation:
I am given, I confess, to exaggeration.

He is fastidious about mobile telephones,
text messages, and much of the twenty-first century.
Bruges is the feudal European past,
where I wouldn't have belonged and which was
never especially kind nor gentle, at least
not in Breughel's vision of the peasantry.

At the Heart of This Black World

after Olga Martynova

What does the river know of its own bed,
Or the spider of the web?

What does a canvas know of a painting?

Who knows what anyone understands or needs?
In this dark abyss, everything
is frightening and gentle at once.

What does the backing cloth know about silk?

We are in a dark, hidden
hollow full of songs, moans, whistling
and the click of fingers.

Listen.

Night Thoughts

after Olga Martynova

Night unwraps the true stuff of the world:
Poorly clothed houses, shadows in a back street,
Lorries and lime trees on the boulevards –
Faces show bewildered discontent. What still holds
Of their comfortable life? Is this new look
Deception or reality? Electric words
Suddenly flash their alphabet. Night
Moves, lit only by itself. And until
The light of early morning, you can
Repeat the letters of the night-time world.
Now, a sign flashes in a passing headlight,
Then somebody's whisper, menacing footsteps,
God knows what else – as the black scene shines.
Day clothes this nakedness and
Hides the evidence of it within our flesh.
Language turns into babble, and then,
Sitting on a bench in the boulevard
You try helplessly to remember what remains
Once night has gone, more than
A worn-out negative of how things are
Under the heels of the rain.

London

for Natasha

A full ginger moon hangs in the garden.
On this side of the house there are no stars.
When I go to bed, I like to soothe myself with
streetlights, lit windows and passing cars.

When my grandchild comes to sleep over
I find we share the same preference.
She doesn't want to draw the curtains either.
I like to look out on my town, my London...

Have you seen London from above? she asks me.
It's like a field of lights. And her grey eyes widen.
Her eight-year-old spirit is tender as blossom.
Be gentle to her now, ferocious London.